SandCastle™

Baby Mammals

It's a Baby

White-Tailed Deer!

Kelly Doudna

Consulting Editor, Diane Craig, M.A./Reading Specialist

ABDO
Publishing Company

Published by ABDO Publishing Company, 8000 West 78th Street, Edina, Minnesota 55439.

Printed in the United States.

Editor: Pam Price
Content Developer: Nancy Tuminelly
Cover and Interior Design and Production: Mighty Media
Photo Credits: Eyewire, Peter Arnold Inc. (John Cancalosi, S.J. Krasemann, Bruce Lichtenberger, Carl R. Sams II, Diane Shapiro, Tom Vezo, R. Wittek), ShutterStock

Library of Congress Cataloging-in-Publication Data

Doudna, Kelly, 1963-
 It's a baby white-tailed deer! / Kelly Doudna.
  p. cm. -- (Baby mammals)
 ISBN 978-1-60453-033-9
 1. White-tailed deer--Infancy--Juvenile literature. I. Title.

QL737.U55D68 2008
599.65'2139--dc22
                    2007033746

SandCastle™ Level: Fluent

SandCastle™ books are created by a team of professional educators, reading specialists, and content developers around five essential components—phonemic awareness, phonics, vocabulary, text comprehension, and fluency—to assist young readers as they develop reading skills and strategies and increase their general knowledge. All books are written, reviewed, and leveled for guided reading, early reading intervention, and Accelerated Reader® programs for use in shared, guided, and independent reading and writing activities to support a balanced approach to literacy instruction. The SandCastle™ series has four levels that correspond to early literacy development. The levels are provided to help teachers and parents select appropriate books for young readers.

Emerging Readers
(no flags)

Beginning Readers
(1 flag)

Transitional Readers
(2 flags)

Fluent Readers
(3 flags)

SandCastle™ would like to hear from you. Please send us your comments and suggestions.
sandcastle@abdopublishing.com

Vital Statistics

for the White-Tailed Deer

BABY NAME
fawn

NUMBER IN LITTER
1 to 4, average 2

WEIGHT AT BIRTH
4 to 8 pounds

AGE OF INDEPENDENCE
1 year for males, 2 years for females

ADULT WEIGHT
90 to 220 pounds

LIFE EXPECTANCY
2 to 3 years

A white-tailed deer doe gives birth to one or two fawns. Fawns are able to walk within minutes of being born.

Some does may have three or four fawns.

Fawns have many white spots in their coats. The spots help the fawns blend in with their surroundings.

Fawns lie flat on the ground while their mothers are away eating. Fawns stay very still so they don't attract predators.

Predators of the deer include wolves, coyotes, and mountain lions.

A deer relies mainly on its sense of smell to detect predators.

Deer also have very good senses of sight and hearing.

Deer usually escape from predators by running away. But deer are also good swimmers.

Deer live in most areas of North America. They prefer woodsy or bushy habitats.

Deer are herbivores. They eat any plants they can find.

Fawns lose their spots when they grow their first winter coats. They are about five months old when this happens.

Male fawns leave their mothers when they are one year old. Female fawns stay until they are two.

Fun Fact

About the White-Tailed Deer

Deer are fast runners. They can sprint at speeds up to 30 miles per hour. That's about the same speed that cars move in the city.

SPEED LIMIT 30

Glossary

detect – to discover or find out about.

expectancy – an expected or likely amount.

habitat – the area or environment where a person or thing usually lives.

herbivore – an animal that eats mainly plants.

independence – the state of no longer needing others to care for or support you.

predator – an animal that hunts others.

rely – to trust or depend on.

sprint – to run as fast as possible for a short distance.

To see a complete list of SandCastle™ books and other nonfiction titles from ABDO Publishing Company, visit **www.abdopublishing.com**.

8000 West 78th Street, Edina, MN 55439

800-800-1312 • 952-831-1632 fax